D1517527

SPACE!

ASTEROIDS, METEORS, AND COMETS

JOSEPHA SHERMAN

Marshall Cavendish
Benchmark
New York

Marshall Cavendish Benchmark
99 White Plains Road
Tarrytown, New York 10591
www.marshallcavendish.us

All Websites were available and accurate when this book was sent to press.

Editor: Karen Ang
Publisher: Michelle Bisson
Art Director: Anahid Hamparian
Series design by Daniel Roode
Production by nSight Inc

Library of Congress Cataloging-in-Publication Data

Sherman, Josepha.
   Asteroids, meteors, and comets / by Josepha Sherman.
      p. cm. -- (Space!)
   Summary: "Describes asteroids, meteors, and comets, including their histories, their
compositions, and their roles in the solar system"--Provided by publisher.
   Includes bibliographical references and index.
   ISBN 978-0-7614-4252-3
   1. Asteroids--Juvenile literature. 2. Meteors--Juvenile literature. 3.
Comets--Juvenile literature. I. Title.
   QB651.S497 2010
   523.44--dc22
   20080372815

Front cover: An asteroid and a comet.
Title page: A meteor streaking through Earth's atmosphere.
Front cover: Steve A. Munsinger / Photo Researchers Inc.
Photo research by Candlepants, Inc.
The photographs in this book are used by permission and through the courtesy of:
Getty Images: Pete Turner, 1; Kauko Helavuo, 4, 5; Harvey Lloyd, 16; AFP, 20, 24; Roger
Viollet, 30; Roger Ressmeyer, 45. NASA: 7, 52; JPL/JHUAPL, 8, 18, 46; Lunar and Planetary
Institute, 13; JPL/USGS, 17; Mount Wilson and Las Campanas Observatories of the
Carnegie Institute of Washington, 44; JPL/UMD, 57; ESA, 58. Photo Researchers Inc.:
Henning Dalhoff / Bonnier Publications, 10; Joe Tucciarone, 14; Science Source, 31; Frank
Zullo, 38; Royal Astronomical Society, 40, 42; Shigemi Numazawa / Atlas Photo Bank, 47.
AP Images: John Raoux, 21; 27; HO, 50; Michael Sohn, 56. Alamy Images: Scott Camazine,
25; Images of Africa Photobank, 28; Phototake Inc., 53. Corbis: Jonathan Blair, 22, 23; ALI
JAREKJI/Reuters, 33; Roger Ressmeyer, 34, 35. The Image Works: Mary Evans Picture
Library, 37.

Printed in Malaysia
123456

CONTENTS

1

WHAT IS AN ASTEROID?

Until the beginning of the nineteenth century, nobody really knew about **asteroids**. Most asteroids were too small to be seen by the telescopes of the time. No one even had a suspicion that they were there, until one man happened to be looking at the right place at the right time.

EARLY DISCOVERIES

Giuseppe Piazzi was an Italian monk who was very interested in mathematics and astronomy. Piazzi set up an observatory in Palermo, Italy, where he felt the southern location and calm weather would offer clear views of the sky. Using a telescope,

Asteroids have most likely been moving around in space since our Solar System was formed. Their distance from Earth, however, made it hard for early astronomers to identify them.

Piazzi started making his observations in 1791. While examining the sky, Piazzi realized that star charts—the maps and drawings of the stars in the sky—were very outdated. He decided to update them based on his observations.

On January 1, 1801, Piazzi found an unexpected "star" in the sky. At first, he was unsure, writing that, "I have announced this star as a **comet**, but since it is not accompanied by any [cloudy light] . . . and, further, since its movement is so slow and rather uniform . . . it might be something better than a comet." The object was soon lost in the glare of the Sun. Piazzi asked a mathematician, Carl Friedrich Gauss, to help him locate this new object. Gauss developed a new method of **orbit** calculation—which figured out the path the object was taking. Gauss's calculations worked and astronomers were able to locate the object again. After its orbit was better determined, it was clear

HONORED IN THE TWENTIETH CENTURY

As more asteroids were discovered, they were given numbers along with names. In 1923, the one thousandth asteroid to be named was called 1000 Piazzia in honor of Piazzi. Because of his accomplishments in astronomy, a large crater on Ceres—revealed by the Hubble Space Telescope—was named Piazzi.

that this object was not a comet. It appeared to be a small planet between Mars and Jupiter.

Piazzi wanted to call his find Ceres Ferdinandea, "Ceres" for the Roman goddess of the crops and "Ferdinandea" after King Ferdinand of Sicily. The object—which was later determined to be an asteroid—eventually became known simply as Ceres. Piazzi continued to chart the stars, and in 1803, he published a list of 6,784 stars. Then, in 1814, he improved that list and published a new list with 7,646 stars.

From 1801—and Piazzi's discovery of Ceres—to 1807, there were only four asteroid discoveries. After that, no other asteroids were discovered until 1845. As telescopes improved, the number of asteroids discov-

This image of Ceres was taken by the Hubble Space Telescope in 2005, more than two hundred years after Piazzi first discovered it.

ered increased. From 1845 on into the twentieth century, there was at least one—and often more than one—asteroid discovered every year.

Scientists knew that there was much more that could be learned from seeing these asteroids up close. But close-up views had to wait until the end of the twentieth century, until the creation of stronger telescopes and the development of spacecraft that could travel near these asteroids.

ASTEROID ORIGINS

Asteroids are rocky mini-planets, which are sometimes called minor planets or planetoids. Many of them revolve around the Sun in a large orbit between Mars and Jupiter. The **gravity** of the Sun and nearby objects, such as planets, is what keeps the asteroids moving in an orbit.

Asteroids are found in many sizes. Ceres is about 580 miles (933 kilometers) across, and for a long time was known as the largest asteroid. A tiny one, called 1991 BA, is only about 26 feet (6 meters) across. Asteroids can even be so small that telescopes cannot see them.

Close examination of structure and features was only possible when strong telescopes and spacecraft were able to get close to an asteroid. A computerized image of the asteroid Mathilde was created by combining several images taken by the *NEAR* spacecraft in 1997.

CERES, THE DWARF PLANET

Until 2006, Ceres was considered the largest asteroid in the Solar System. That year, the International Astronomical Union (IAU), which is made up of scientists from around the world, defined what a planet was. As a result, Pluto, which had been one of the nine main planets in the Solar System, was reclassified as a dwarf planet. Because of its size and characteristics, Ceres was also changed from an asteroid to a dwarf planet. It is the only dwarf planet found in the asteroid belt between Mars and Jupiter. Most other dwarf planets are much farther from the Sun, beyond Pluto's orbit.

The Formation of the Solar System

Many scientists believe that our Solar System was formed about 4.5 billion years ago. A huge cloud of dust and gas began to form, probably after the massive explosion of a nearby star. The cloud had its own gravitation force and pulled the gas and dust particles together. These particles eventually became so hot that they exploded and began to form the Sun, the star at the center of our Solar System.

As a result of this huge explosion, more gas and dust particles were flung into space. However, they stayed close enough to the Sun to be affected by its gravity. The particles grouped together in a ring that revolved around the Sun. Over the course of about 100,000 years, the particles joined together to form small bodies that eventually became the planets and other **celestial objects** in our Solar System.

The four planets closest to the Sun—Mercury, Venus, Earth, and Mars—are rocky land-based, or terrestrial, planets. The

One theory of Solar System formation states that the planets, moons, and other celestial bodies are formed from the rocks, gases, and dust particles pulled together by the Sun's gravity.

four outer planets (Jupiter, Saturn, Neptune, and Uranus) are gas giants that are mostly made up of gas.

Astronomers have no clear idea of how the asteroids came to be. They think that asteroids might be the remains of planets that never finished forming when the others did, or "leftovers" from the material used to form the Solar System. Most think that the asteroid belt—which lies between Mars, the farthest terrestrial planet, and Jupiter, the closest gas planet—is filled with material left over from the Solar System's formation.

THE ASTEROID BELT

The belt is an unwelcoming place, with massive amounts of debris moving around and extremely cold temperatures. The average surface temperature of an asteroid in the belt is -100 degrees Fahrenheit (-73 degrees Celcius).

At least 750,000 asteroids in the belt are larger than 1 mile (1.5 km) across. More than two hundred asteroids are larger than 60 miles (100 km) across. Scientists believe that there are probably millions of smaller asteroids that are too small to see with telescopes and other space observation equipment.

In 2005, scientists discovered what they believe is another asteroid belt that orbits a star named HD 69830. This star, which is more than 40 **light-years** away from our Solar System, has some qualities similar to our Sun. The asteroid belt that orbits this star is larger than the one in our Solar System and has more asteroids. More research and observations will need to be made, but many scientists are excited by this discovery. If asteroid belts hold the remains—or maybe even the beginnings—of planetary formation, then perhaps more planets are developing around far-off stars. Some scientists also think that since HD 69830 is similar to our Sun, Earth-like planets may form near it.

CLASSIFYING ASTEROIDS

Astronomers now classify, or divide, asteroids in the belt into two broad groups based on their composition, or makeup. One group of asteroids dominates the outer part of the asteroid belt between Mars and Jupiter. These asteroids are rich in the element carbon. Scientist believe that the composition of these asteroids has not changed much since the Solar System formed. Asteroids in the second group, in the inner part of the belt, are rich in minerals. These asteroids are much younger and probably formed from melted materials as the Solar System was being formed.

Most asteroids follow elliptical or oval-shaped orbits in the asteroid belt. Some groups of asteroids follow the same orbit. These groups are called Hirayama families. The name comes from Kiyotsugu Hirayama, the Japanese astronomer who first discovered them.

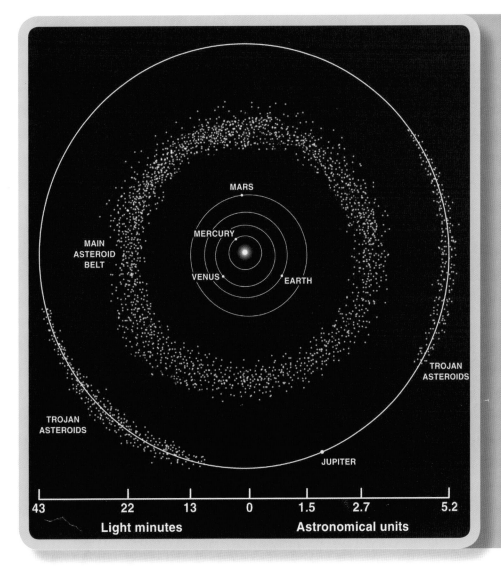

MARS

MERCURY

MAIN
ASTEROID
BELT

VENUS

EARTH

TROJAN
ASTEROIDS

TROJAN
ASTEROIDS

JUPITER

| 43 | 22 | 13 | 0 | 1.5 | 2.7 | 5.2 |
| **Light minutes** | | | | **Astronomical units** | | |

An illustration shows the different parts of the Solar System where most asteroids can be found.

Though most of the known asteroids are in the belt between Mars and Jupiter, many follow orbits outside the belt. For example, a number of asteroids called Trojans follow the same orbit as Jupiter. Astronomers think that Neptune may also have its own collection of Trojan asteroids.

EARTH-CROSSING ASTEROIDS

The asteroid belt or the orbits of other planets are not the only places where asteroids can be found. There are unknown numbers of wandering asteroids. Some of these move outside of their orbits, are drawn in by an object's gravity, and crash

This illustration shows what an asteroid might have looked like as it entered Earth's atmosphere and headed toward the planet's surface.

into it. This is one reason why many planets and moons have irregular or dented surfaces.

Hundreds of asteroids regularly cut across Earth's orbit. These are called **Earth-crossing asteroids**. While most of these never come close enough to cause any problems, some have actually hit our planet in the past. The very small ones—most likely pebble-sized by the time they reach land—just disappear into the soil. But if asteroids larger than 1 mile (1.6 km) across hit Earth at high speeds, they could do serious damage.

Many scientists believe that the Chicxulub Crater in the Yucatan Peninsula of Mexico is the site of an asteroid impact that happened 65 million years ago. They believe that it caused massive environmental changes, including a seemingly endless darkness and winter. Known as the K-T event, scientists think that it led to massive extinctions throughout Earth, including most of the dinosaurs.

Another site of an asteroid impact is in Arizona. Thousands of years ago, an asteroid that was probably about 200 feet (61 m) across hit the planet. The impact was so hard that the asteroid ended up buried deep in the ground. The impact site is known as Barringer Crater, or Meteor Crater, and is nearly 1 mile (1.6 km) across.

In January 2006, scientists studying a dust layer buried deep in the ground announced that it had been created sometime

The massive impact from an asteroid crashing into Earth caused a deep crater that is almost a mile wide.

in the last 80 million years. An asteroid probably broke apart in space and created a blanket of dust over much of the Earth.

There are still many other Earth-crossing asteroids in space. But is Earth in any danger? Earth has been hit by asteroids in the past and probably will be struck again. Some strikes may be small and unnoticeable. As for the larger, more dangerous ones, scientist hope that in the future improved technology will helps us predict and reroute or destroy any dangerous asteroids heading too close to our planet.

ASTEROIDS OBSERVED

When humans started launching spacecraft, the missions were usually focused on traveling to and observing moons or planets.

Finding out more about asteroids was usually just an added bonus. As scientists learned more, however, space missions and special technology were developed specifically to learn about the asteroids in our Solar System.

Galileo and Gaspra

The first close-up image of an asteroid was taken by the *Galileo* spacecraft in 1991. The *Galileo* mission was part of the United States' space program, which is run by the **National Aeronautics and Space Administration (NASA)**. Although *Galileo*'s main mission was to study Jupiter, it did fly close enough to an asteroid named Gaspra to take its picture. Gaspra looks a little like a crater-pitted football. It is fairly small for an asteroid—about 11 miles (18 km) by 6.5 miles (10.5 km). Scientists suspect it may be a fragment of some larger object, broken off in some collision. It may also have later been hit by another asteroid that left Gaspra ridged or grooved.

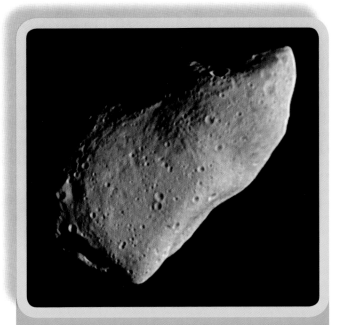

The *Galileo* spacecraft was able to take several clear images of the asteroid Gaspra in 1991.

Near-Earth Asteroid Rendezvous (NEAR) Shoemaker

This NASA spacecraft was launched on February 17, 1996. *NEAR*'s mission was to make successful visits to two asteroids—243 Mathilde and 433 Eros, which are two **near-Earth asteroids**. The *NEAR* spacecraft made a successful **flyby** of asteroid 243 Mathilde on June 27, 1997, sending back data to the scientists on Earth.

The images from *NEAR* show several large craters that were probably caused when other asteroids crashed into 243 Mathilde. Scientists suspect that 243 Mathilde survived the impact because it seems to be a collection of rocks clinging together by gravity rather than one solid rock. They theorize that if 243 Mathilde was a solid-rock asteroid, it would have broken apart with the hard impact.

On December 23, 1998, *NEAR* made its second successful flyby, this time by the 433 Eros asteroid. After doing its flyby, the spacecraft was supposed to return to 433 Eros and orbit the asteroid. However, there was a problem with the main engine and *NEAR* kept on going past

The *NEAR* spacecraft provided scientists with a close look at 433 Eros's strange shape.

Eros. Scientists back on Earth eventually managed to get *NEAR* back on course. On February 14, 2000, the spacecraft went into orbit around 433 Eros. A series of careful maneuvers put the spacecraft closer to the asteroid. During the summer of 2000, the spacecraft spent several weeks in a nearly circular orbit around 433 Eros. *NEAR* was only 21.5 miles (35 km) from the asteroid's surface. Observations of the asteroid show that it is odd-looking and not round like other asteroids. Scientists think that 433 Eros was hit hard by another asteroid, which is what caused its strange shape and its oddly smooth surface.

Hayabusa

On May 9, 2003, JAXA, the Japanese space agency, launched the *Hayabusa* spacecraft. Its mission was to fly to the asteroid Itokawa, map it, land on it, and take samples. However, space is an unpredictable environment. While *Hayabusa* was on its way to Itokawa, a large and unexpected solar flare, or outburst from the Sun, damaged the spacecraft. Since the spacecraft was already far from Earth, there was nothing the scientists could do but wait and watch. As a result of the damage, the spacecraft's speed was reduced. Instead of reaching Itokawa in June 2005, *Hayabusa* arrived in September 2005. In order to complete its mission, *Hayabusa* had to leave the asteroid by November. This late arrival decreased the amount of time the spacecraft had to study the asteroid.

Japan's *Hayabusa* spacecraft sent back images of the bean-shaped Itokawa asteroid (left) and its surface (right). *Hayabusa* is scheduled to return to Earth in 2010.

That was not the only problem. Just after the *Hayabusa* finished mapping the asteroid, two of its thruster systems failed. In addition, the sampling attempt failed. But the *Hayabusa* did take some excellent images of the asteroid and made excellent maps. *Hayabusa*'s images revealed that Itokawa has a surface covered with rocky boulders and giant rock splinters. There are no impact craters. Scientists believe Itokawa is a "rubble-pile" asteroid, which is made up of a loose collection of fractured rocks and dust.

Dawn

Launched by NASA on September 27, 2007, *Dawn* is on a mission to the two most massive members of the asteroid belt: Ceres and the asteroid Vesta. *Dawn* is scheduled to explore Vesta between 2011 and 2012 and Ceres in 2015. It will be the first spacecraft to visit either body.

These missions, along with others and careful telescopic observations, have given scientist a great deal of information about asteroids. As of 2008, there are 187,745 known and named asteroids, with so many more yet to be discovered. Space agencies around the world will most likely plan more asteroid-focused space missions. It may even be possible that NASA could land astronauts on Ceres in 2025.

Engineers prepare the *Dawn* spacecraft before its 2007 launch.

2

METEOROIDS, METEORS, AND METEORITES

s Earth moves through its orbit, celestial objects or space debris—extra material—can enter the planet's atmosphere. Smaller rocks and dust particles that travel through the atmosphere often appear as "shooting stars." These rocks are called **meteors**. (Before they enter the atmosphere, they are called **meteoroids**.) Meteors can come from different celestial objects. For example, many small Earth-crossing asteroids are small enough to be pulled to Earth by the planet's gravity. Once they enter the atmosphere, these small asteroids become meteors.

Meteorites come in many shapes and sizes and are collected by scientist and non-scientists around the world. The minerals in this meteorite make the rock glow when light shines behind it.

Meteors that flash through the sky during a meteor shower, such as the Leonids shown here, may look like colorful streaks lighting up the night.

Meteoroids and meteors can range in size. Many are only inches in size. Meteors travel at high speeds—sometimes as fast as 45,000 miles (72,404 km) per hour. When the meteor burns up in the atmosphere, it produces streaks or balls of light that seem to shoot across the sky.

Sometimes groups of meteors enter and move through Earth's atmosphere. This is called a **meteor shower**. A meteor shower usually occurs when Earth passes through the path of a comet. The comet has left behind dust, particles, and rocks. These rocks and particles turn into meteors when they enter and burn up in Earth's atmosphere.

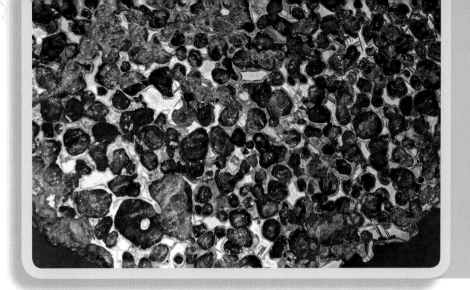

A stony iron meteorite is made up of rocks, minerals, and metallic elements combined together in space.

Because of their size and the amount of heat and energy created when they move through Earth's atmosphere, most meteors burn up and disintegrate before they hit the planet's surface. Every now and then, however, a meteor survives its blazing journey toward Earth and actually hits the ground. Once it is on the ground, it is called a **meteorite**. Meteorites can be found all over the planet. Most meteorites are made of stone, iron, nickel, or a mix of different metallic elements. The majority of meteorites are as small as pebbles, but some can be huge boulder-sized chunks of space rock.

SIGHTINGS

Throughout history, meteor sightings and meteorite discoveries have been recorded around the world. Pliny the Elder of ancient Rome was a scientist who wrote about a meteorite that fell in Greece in 467 BCE. He described it as being as large as a wagon

METEORITE TOOLS AND WEAPONS

Historians note that early people who lived in the region that is now known as Greenland discovered at least eight iron meteorites. Though the people probably did not know that these metallic rocks came from space, they found uses for them. By the seventeenth century, when Europeans traveled to that region, the local people were seen using tools and weapons edged with iron from the meteorites.

and brown in color. Pliny also recorded eyewitness accounts of "a vast, fiery body" in the sky, but added that "when it afterwards came down to the ground . . . there was no fire . . . only a [big] stone."

Asia and Africa

In China, as far back as the Chou Dynasty—about 3,000 years ago—weapons were being forged, or made, from iron meteorites. One of the earliest historical accounts of a meteorite strike comes from Japan. A meteorite fell on the grounds of a Shinto temple on May 19, 861 CE. On Java—an island in Indonesia—several royal swords from the eighteenth century were forged from iron meteorites.

Fewer meteorites have been found in Africa. However, the Mbosi meteorite is about 16 tons (14.5 tonnes) and landed in the

The sword on the right was created in 1290 and is made with meteorite steel from the Middle East.

area that is now Tanzania. The local people felt that the meteorite should not be touched or its metal used. The largest meteorite found in one piece is located in Namibia. The Hoba, or Hoba West, meteorite weighs nearly 60 tons (54 tonnes). Scientists think that the meteorite probably landed on Earth about 80,000 years ago. Unlike some other meteorite impacts, the Hoba meteorite seems to have landed without causing a large crater or surrounding damage. Scientists think this might be because the meteor was slowed down by Earth's thick atmosphere.

The area around the Hoba meteorite was excavated so that scientists could study the rock, but the meteorite was too large and heavy to move.

The Americas

In the past, many people probably understood that these rocks had come from the sky, but had no way of knowing from how far away those odd stones had come or what they were. The Aztec people who lived in Mexico hundreds of years ago had their own beliefs about meteor showers and meteorites. One of the Aztecs' surviving manuscripts mentions a meteorite strike. There is a reference to an animal wounded by a "shooting star," saying that it was not to be eaten. A reference to a meteor shower describes everyone protecting themselves at night, covering themselves completely for fear of being hit by one of those shooting stars.

Fewer meteorites have been found in South America. The ones that have been discovered are considered sacred objects. The Patagonian people at the southern tip of Argentina felt that the 254-pound (115-kilogram) Caperr iron meteorite should not be touched.

The Hopewell lived in North America more than a thousand years ago. Historians discovered that the Hopewell who lived in what is now Ohio and Kansas found and used meteorites. The Hopewell created a trade route along various rivers, trading beads and chips made of metallic rocks for whatever supplies they needed. The metallic rocks came from what is now referred to as the Brenham meteorite. It landed in the area that now includes Kansas.

The Willamette iron meteorite landed in the region that now includes Oregon thousands of years ago. It weighs more than 15 tons (13.6 tonnes). The Clackamas natives believed that it would give strength to anyone who washed his face in the rainwater that collected in the rock's holes. Warriors would dip their arrowheads in the water for added power. The Willamette meteorite is the largest meteor ever found in the United States. It is on display in the American Museum of Natural History in New York.

This image of the Willamette meteorite was taken around 1910, when it was displayed at the Natural History Museum in New York.

Another giant meteorite landed in what is now Arizona. Weighing nearly 2 tons (1.8 tonnes), it was considered a sacred object of the Dine, or Navajo people. The meteorite is now in the Field Museum of Natural History in Chicago and is called the Navajo Meteorite.

Not all meteor impacts occurred thousands of years ago. On April 24, 2005, at 10:10 PM, citizens of Branford, Connecticut, saw what they thought was a plane crashing into Long Island Sound.

THE MURCHISON METEORITE

In September 28, 1969, people who lived near Murchison, Australia, saw a fireball shoot through the sky before it broke into pieces and disappeared. Shortly after that, they felt the ground shake as the meteorite struck. This meteorite was called the Murchison meteorite and is actually a group of small pieces of one large meteorite. Scientists continue to be fascinated by this meteorite because it is not like most meteorites. Instead of being mostly made up of nickel and iron, this meteorite has a lot of carbon-based elements from space. Many scientists think that studying the Murchison Meteorite will help give them clues about the Solar System and how it formed.

A scientists tests a part of the Murchison meteorite.

Fortunately, it turned out to be a small meteor making a splash-down landing.

On February 20, 2008, at 1:45 AM, residents of Spokane, Washington, saw and heard a meteor streaking through the sky. People reported seeing bright lights and hearing loud booms in parts of Washington, Oregon, and Idaho. The Federal Aviation Administration (FAA) also received reports by pilots in the region who had seen the meteor streak by them. The meteor has yet to be found. Many people think that it is probably somewhere in the Idaho wilderness.

METEOR SHOWERS

Many people—not just astronomers—enjoy watching meteor showers light up the night sky. Most can be seen without the aid of binoculars or a telescope. Some showers appear every year and last for several days, though peak viewing time may be on a specific evening, depending upon where a person lives.

The Perseids

Like all meteor showers, the Perseid meteor shower gets its name from the constellation—or group of stars—near the place where the meteors seem to originate. For example, the Leonid meteor shower originates near the Leo constellation. In the case of the Perseid meteors—or Perseids, for short—the Perseus constellation is the shower's origin. The Perseids is one of the most famous meteor showers because it is easy for astronomers and non-astronomers to see in the night sky.

Every year, people living in the Northern Hemisphere tend to have better views of the Perseids, which can last from the end of July to nearly the end of August. The Perseids appear to be the fastest moving meteor shower, with many bright lights streaking the sky every minute. Historians believe that people have been observing the Perseids since at least the eighth century.

The Perseid meteor shower is a result of Earth passing through debris left by the Comet Swift-Tuttle.

3
COMETS

t is likely that comets have been observed for as long as people looked to the skies. The Babylonian people who lived in the land that is now present-day Iraq kept careful astronomical notes. A comet was seen streaking across the sky from June to July of 210 BCE. In 164 BCE, it is possible that the Babylonians caught a glimpse of the comet that is now called Halley's Comet.

The earliest Chinese mention of a comet comes from 1059 BCE, when a comet was witnessed during a war between King Wu-Wang and King Chou. There are records of regular comet sightings from that date on. For example, the comet that was seen in 467 BCE was actually the same meteorite that Pliny the Elder recorded as falling in Greece. Throughout the centuries, Chinese astronomers made several notes of the regular reappearances of Halley's Comet.

Halley's Comet is probably the most famous comet. It has been noted in the sky over the course of nearly two thousand years.

A book from around 168 BCE includes a listing of comets and what their appearance meant. For example, Chi-Guan was a comet with a tail that looked like a spear. To the Chinese, this meant that war was coming or that a general would die. Pu-Hui, a comet with a triple tail, meant disease would soon strike.

In ancient Greek folk belief, comets were evil signs of bad news. During the winter of 373 to 372 BCE, a comet was seen during a great earthquake and tidal wave in Greece. Occurrences like these strengthened the beliefs that comets were bad. However, some Greek scholars were more interested in finding out what comets actually were.

Aristotle was a Greek scholar who studied and wrote about many different subjects. One of the books he wrote was called *Meteorologica*. It was about his observations of comets, together with the thoughts of other scholars. Aristotle refused to accept any theories he thought were foolish, such as the idea that there was only one comet and that it was a planet. In his book, Aristotle also includes debates about comet tails and whether they were made of moisture drawn from the planets the comet passed. Some scholars claimed that comets were just an optical illusion caused by the planets. Aristotle argued that comets were seen where there were no planets. Aristotle thought that comets were not solid, but were caused by warm air in the upper sky colliding with the cold air of outer space, triggering a fireball.

Many people believed that comets were either warnings of bad news or marked some major changes about to happen. Comets were often tied to famous births or deaths.

Seneca was a Roman teacher and writer who lived from around 4 BCE to 65 CE. Seneca wrote a book called *Naturales Quaestiones*, or *Natural Questions,* about astronomy and meteorology, which is the study of the weather. Seneca included observations from earlier scholars, but he concluded that, "Nature . . . does not often display comets; she has assigned them a different place, different periods from the other stars and motions unlike theirs. . . ." Seneca also believed that people should have a clear record of all comet appearances—from the past to the present—so that scientists could have accurate records.

One of the first Europeans to study comets was

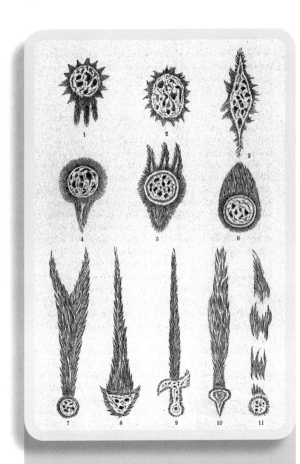

These illustrations of different types of comets were created from Pliny the Elder's observations.

the English priest known as the Venerable (a title meaning "Respected") Bede. Bede lived from about 673 CE to 735 CE. Like most of the people of his time, he believed that comets were signs of change. However, Bede also made careful observations of the comets, where they appeared most often, how they looked, and how they moved.

Petroglyphs, or pictographs, carved into rocks by ancient people, such as the Hohokam, represent different celestial bodies. For example, experts believe that the netlike grid pattern represents the Milky Way galaxy, and the image on its lower left could be a comet.

Early peoples who lived in the Americas also observed comets as they moved across the sky. The Anasazi people lived in the region of present-day Arizona that includes Chaco Canyon during about the sixth to the thirteenth or fourteenth centuries. Though they left no written records, they did leave pictographs—stone carvings—showing an exploding star. Scientists and historians have since determined that this exploding star was a supernova in the Crab Nebula that exploded around 1054 CE. Below the pictograph of the supernova is a picture of a comet. Historians believe that this is probably proof that the Anasazi witnessed Halley's Comet, which appeared in 1066.

The Hohokam lived in southern Arizona at about the same time as the Anasazi and made pictographs of their comet sightings. The pictograph they made shows the symbol for a star with a tail below it. This may also be a representation of Halley's Comet's 1066 appearance. Other early Natives, such as the Coco, also left pictograph records of comet sightings.

NEW DISCOVERIES

The seventeenth century brought about renewed interest in astronomy as more powerful telescopes were created. Better technology allowed scientists to look farther into space. For the first time, they could make more accurate calculations and descriptions of once-mysterious celestial objects.

Edmond Halley and His Comet

Edmond Halley was born in London in 1656. While attending Oxford University, Halley met John Flamsteed, the top astronomer of England. When he saw that Flamsteed was compiling an accurate catalog of the stars of the Northern Hemisphere, Halley decided to do the same thing for the stars of the Southern Hemisphere. His star catalog was the first to show star locations determined completely by telescope.

On November 22, 1682, Halley had seen a comet that had triggered his interest. Years later he wondered whether or not the comet he had seen had visited Earth before and whether it would return again. To figure this out, he needed to calculate the

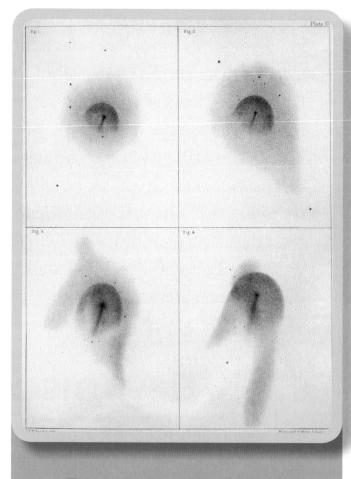

The astronomer William Herschel drew these sketches of Halley's Comet as he observed it in 1835.

positions of Earth, Jupiter, and Saturn, and where the comet would be in relation to them. It took Halley more than twenty years, but in 1705, he felt confident enough to write, "Now many things lead me to believe that the comet of the year 1531 . . . is the same as that which in the year 1607, was described . . . which I saw and observed myself at its return in 1682." In Halley's *A Synopsis of the Astronomy of Comets*, he describes the orbits of twenty-four comets that had been observed from 1337 to 1698. He showed that the three historic comets of 1531, 1607, and 1682 were so similar in characteristics that they must have been the same comet that kept returning. He also accurately predicted that the comet would return in 1758. That comet was named Halley's Comet in his honor.

Caroline Herschel's Comets

Caroline Herschel was the sister of astronomer William Herschel, who had made many discoveries, including the planet Uranus. Caroline was an excellent astronomer, as well, and worked with her brother and on her own. She specialized in finding comets and discovered several.

The first of Herschel's comet discoveries was on August 1, 1786. This comet is known now as Comet C/1786 P1 (Herschel). The second of Caroline Herschel's comet discoveries was made on December 21, 1788. She shared this discovery with French astronomer Roger Rigolett, so the comet is now called Comet 35P/

Herschel-Rigollet. The third and fourth comet discoveries came in 1790. There was Comet C/1790 A1 (Herschel) on January 7, and Comet C/1790 H1 (Herschel) on April 18. Her fifth comet was found on December 15, 1791, and has been named Comet C/1791 X1 (Herschel). The last comet that Caroline Herschel discovered was found on August 14, 1797. It was a joint discovery with French astronomer Eugene Bovard, so the comet is officially known as Comet C/1797 P1 (Bouvard-Herschel).

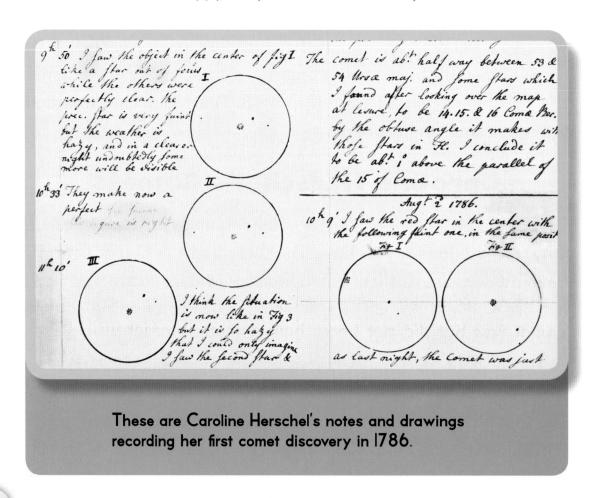

These are Caroline Herschel's notes and drawings recording her first comet discovery in 1786.

MARIA MITCHELL

On October 1, 1847, American astronomer Maria Mitchell, who lived on Nantucket Island off Massachusetts, discovered a new comet that scientists named after her. In 1848 she was elected to the American Academy of Arts—the first woman to be so honored. Frederick VI, the King of Denmark, who was interested in astronomy, awarded her a gold medal for her discovery.

THE TWENTIETH CENTURY

The twentieth century brought about great improvements in ground-based telescopes. However, space science was still fairly new, and the average person was not as knowledgeable about space objects as astronomers and other scientists. Unfortunately, this often led to misunderstandings and misinformation about what was happening in space and what could happen on Earth.

One example is the panic of 1910. Most people knew what a comet was but did not know how comets interact with Earth. When Halley's Comet returned in 1910, scientists predicted that the comet's tail would brush Earth. This terrified many people because they were sure that the tail was poisonous and would cause many problems. The comet came and went, and no one was poisoned.

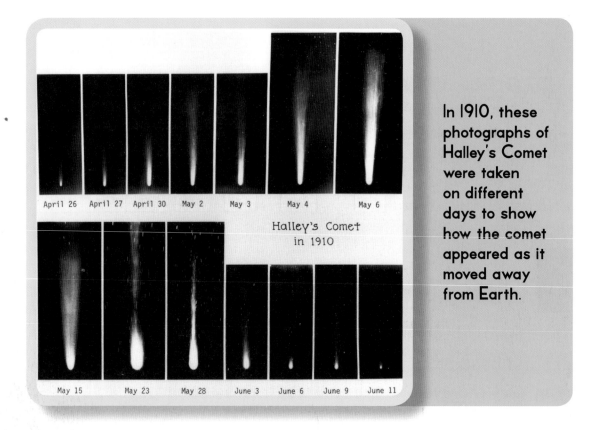

April 26   April 27   April 30   May 2   May 3   May 4   May 6

Halley's Comet
in 1910

May 15   May 23   May 28   June 3   June 6   June 9   June 11

In 1910, these photographs of Halley's Comet were taken on different days to show how the comet appeared as it moved away from Earth.

Fortunately, as time passed, the general public learned more about space science. By the end of the century, space science was being taught in schools across North America and Europe. There were also several space agencies set up to study astronomy and to send out spacecraft to do close observations. Two of the most well-known are the United States' space agency, the National Aeronautics and Space Administration (NASA) and the multi-nation European Space Agency (ESA). Other space programs around the world also work to increase our knowledge of space and all of its many fascinating wonders.

WHAT IS A COMET?

As technology improved and knowledge about space science increased, scientists were able to clearly define many celestial objects, such as comets. Scientists believe that there are around 100 million comets in the Solar System. Astronomers sometimes call comets "dirty snowballs" or "icy mudballs." These odd names come from the comets' makeup. Comets are basically made of a mix of ice—water ice or frozen gases—and space dust.

Comets can be described as having two main parts—the nucleus, or hard center, and the tail, which may extend out for millions of miles. The nucleus is made up of frozen gas, ice, dust, and some rocks. The tails are usually created when the comet moves too close to the Sun. As a result, some of the comet's frozen material changes to gas. The gas trails behind the moving comet.

Hale-Bopp is one of the only comets found to have two tails.

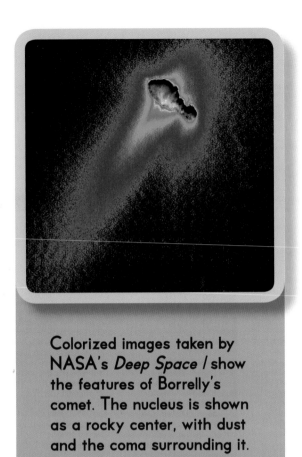

Colorized images taken by NASA's *Deep Space I* show the features of Borrelly's comet. The nucleus is shown as a rocky center, with dust and the coma surrounding it.

Scientists divide a comet into five specific parts: the nucleus, the coma, the hydrogen cloud, the dust tail, and the ion tail. The coma is a dense cloud made up of carbon dioxide, water, and some other gases that come from the nucleus. All comets give off a large, but thin cloud of hydrogen that surrounds the comet. The dust tail is the part of the tail that is made up of dust particles, making it the most visible part to people on Earth who are looking at a comet without telescopes. The ion tail is the gassy part of the tail.

Like planets and other celestial bodies, comets follow a regular orbit around the Sun. However, the length of each comet's orbit can vary. Comets can be divided into two types: long-period and short-period comets.

Comets that take more than 200 years to complete the trip around the Sun are called long-period comets. Some long-period comets can take as long as 30 million years to orbit the Sun. Short-period comets make a complete orbit around the Sun in 200 years or less. Halley's Comet is an example of a short-period comet. It comes close enough to Earth for us to view it every seventy-five to seventy-six years. One group of short-period comets has an orbital period of less than twenty years. These comets are pulled into the inner Solar System by Jupiter's gravity, so they are called Jupiter Family comets.

COMET ORIGINS

One of the big mysteries about comets was their place of origin. In 1950, Dutch astronomer Jan Oort presented the idea that there was an immense cloud surrounding our Solar System. This cloud is more than 18 trillion miles (30 trillion km) from

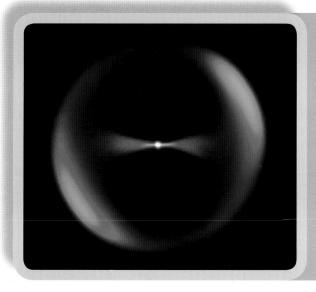

Though they cannot see it because it is so far away, scientists believe that the Oort Cloud looks like a large spherelike structure that surrounds our Solar System.

the Sun. Within the cloud are unknown numbers of comets. One estimate places the number at six trillion, or even higher.

Because the comets are so far from the Sun, they are only weakly held by its gravity. As a result, comets can be influenced by the gravity of other celestial bodies, such as planets, moons, or even other comets. This kind of gravitational pull can change a comet's orbit and send it into our Solar System. Some comets can even move out into the space far beyond our Solar System. Astronomers after Oort added to his discoveries and confirmed the presence of the cloud. To honor Oort's original discovery, the cloud has been named the Oort Cloud.

CLOSE ENCOUNTERS WITH COMETS

The first time a spacecraft came close to a comet was during an international effort between NASA and the ESA. The spacecraft was called the *International Sun-Earth Explorer (ISEE)* and was made up of three satellites. *ISEE-1* and *ISEE-3* were managed by NASA, and *ISEE-2* was managed by the ESA. *ISEE-1* and *ISEE-2* were launched on October 22, 1977, and *ISEE-3* was launched on August 12, 1978. The satellites' main mission was to study the Sun and Earth from space.

After the original studies of the Sun and Earth were completed in 1982, NASA renamed *ISEE-3*. Its new name was *ICE,* or the

International Cometary Explorer. It was sent to intercept the comet P/Giacobini-Zinner. On September 11, 1985, it flew through the tail of the comet. The mission proved that comets are composed of mixed rock and ice. *ICE* is now in an orbit that will bring it close to Earth in 2014. At that time, it may be captured, brought back to Earth, and displayed at the Smithsonian Institution in Washington, D.C.

The Halley Armada

In 1985, Halley's Comet was predicted to pass by Earth. So many nations were interested in studying the comet up close that the series of international spacecraft used were nicknamed the Halley Armada. (An armada is a fleet of ships.) Since space missions are expensive, many of the missions were combined so that more than one goal could be achieved, and scientists from the different nations and organizations shared their findings with each other.

The nations that made up the former Soviet Union were the first to send spacecraft that would study Halley's Comet. *Vega 1* and its twin *Vega 2* were launched from the Baikonur Cosmodrome in December 1984. This was one of the combined missions, aimed to first do a close-up study Venus, and then do a flyby of Halley's Comet. After the spacecraft performed their missions during the Venus flyby in December of 1985, they headed toward Halley's Comet.

On July 2, 1985, the ESA launched the *Giotto* space probe for a close-up look at Halley's Comet. Images started coming back from the *Vega 1* on March 4, 1986, and were used to help pinpoint *Giotto*'s course. On March 6, 1986, *Vega 1* passed near the comet. It was about about 5,524 miles (8,888 km) from the comet's nucleus. On March 9, 1986, *Vega 2* came even closer, at just under 5,000 miles (8,045 km). *Giotto*'s mission was to pass as close as possible to the comet's nucleus, which it did on March 13, 1986. The little spacecraft sent back 2,333 close-up pictures. These included several color photos of the comet's nucleus.

The ESA scientists were sure that the spacecraft would not survive the hits it would receive from comet dust. However, though there was some damage, *Giotto* survived with most of its instruments operating. The mission was extended to allow an encounter with a second comet, Grigg-Skjellerup. In 1992, the probe

One of the first images sent back by *Giotto* shows details of the nucleus of Halley's Comet.

flew by Grigg-Skjellerup and sent back data. Afterward, scientists shut off *Giotto*'s scientific instruments and have left the probe orbiting in space.

In 1985, the Japanese Space Agency—which is now the Japanese Aerospace Exploration Agency (JAXA)—launched its first spacecraft. *Sakigake* was launched from the Kagoshima Space Center and aimed at Halley's Comet. In 1986, it flew by Halley's Comet and was about 4.3 million miles (7 million km) from the comet. A second probe, *Suisei,* was launched on August 18, 1985. It had a double mission: to study Halley's Comet and to measure the solar wind, the flow of particles from the sun. *Suisei* was able to send back several images of the comet.

SHOEMAKER-LEVY 9

Though most comets merely pass by Earth, other planets have experienced comet impacts. On March 23, 1993, three American astronomers discovered a comet orbiting Jupiter. The comet had probably been orbiting the Sun before it was captured by Jupiter's gravity. As the planet's strong gravitation force pulled at it, the comet broke into several smaller pieces. The comet pieces appeared to be lined up like pearls on a string.

The comet was called Shoemaker-Levy 9, after Carolyn and Eugene Shoemaker and David Levy, the astronomers who discovered it. The fragments were expected to crash into Jupiter

A NASA illustration shows what Shoemaker-Levy 9 looked like as it headed toward Jupiter.

around July 1994. This was a huge discovery because it would be the first time in history that people would be able to see a comet hit a planet.

NASA's *Galileo* spacecraft—which had been launched in 1989 to study Jupiter—was able to send back images of the comet's impact. Scientists were astounded by what they saw. Each impact from the fragments was as powerful as hundreds of nuclear bombs exploding. The explosions caused fireballs that were more than 2,000 miles (4,000 km) wide. The impact explosions were so powerful that they scorched, or blackened, Jupiter's outer atmosphere. Scientists guess that if one of those comet fragments had hit Earth, the blast would probably leave behind a crater the size of the state of Rhode Island.

COMET HYAKUTAKE

On January 30, 1996, a Japanese man named Yuji Hyakutake was watching the skies with a pair of strong binoculars. To his surprise and delight, he spotted a comet that was later named after him. Comet Hyakutake never came very close to Earth, but it was visible for a couple of months in 1996.

Astronomers studying the comet suspect that it has not come close to Earth for perhaps thousands of years. They detected chemicals in it that have not been found in other comets. Additionally, the comet seems to be releasing X rays, which are a type of radiation. This is something that has never been observed in other comets. These discoveries make scientists think that this is a new type of comet, one that experienced very different conditions during its formation.

The NASA spacecraft *Ulysses* offered a close look at Comet Hyakutake. *Ulysses* was designed to study the Sun, but passed

Comet Hyakutake was so large and bright that it could be seen with binoculars and regular telescopes.

close to the comet in 1996. The spacecraft's observations noted that Comet Hyakutake has the longest comet tail found yet and proved that a comet tail is made of gas and dust.

COMET HALE-BOPP

Comet Hale-Bopp was discovered separately by two different people on July 23, 1995. As a result, the comet was called Hale-Bopp, after Alan Hale of New Mexico and Thomas Bopp of Arizona. It is the most distant comet discovered by amateur astronomers.

Since its discovery, Hale-Bopp has moved closer to Earth and in early 1997 was expected to make a spectacular appearance. That year, it could be seen from February through December. Hale-Bopp continues to offer surprises to astronomers. Using the Hubble Space Telescope, astronomers have found that the comet has a huge nucleus, estimated to be 19 to 25 miles (30 to 40 km) across. Most comets have a nucleus that measures about 3 miles (5 km) across. Not only is Hale-Bopp's nucleus so large, but it seems to be erupting on itself, spewing out dust from time to time. The comet's surface is also strange because new patches of icy material are regularly brought up to the surface. Scientists are also intrigued by the fact that the comet has water ice in it—as many comets do—but the water ice does not mix with the other icy chemicals and remains separate.

COMET LINEAR

Comet Linear was discovered on September 27, 1999, by the Lincoln Near-Earth Asteroid Research (NEAR) program in New Mexico. It was the NEAR team that combined "Lincoln" with "Near" to get the name "Linear." Linear did not come very close to Earth, but it did get pretty close to the Sun in 2000. ("Close" in this case meant that the comet was still more than 70 million miles [114 km] away.) Scientists do not know if Linear has ever visited our Solar System before or if it will ever return.

However, scientists continue to study the comet. Images from the Hubble Space Telescope revealed interesting things about Linear. On July 5, 2000, the comet blew off a piece of its crust. Astronomers were excited because such eruptions are rare and can tell them more about comet structure.

ONGOING AND FUTURE COMET MISSIONS

Stardust

NASA's *Stardust* spacecraft was launched on February 7, 1999, aiming for Comet Wild 2. It reached the comet on December 31, 2003, and made its closest encounter on January 2, 2004. The main purpose of the mission was to gather samples from the comet. *Stardust* also took seventy-two pictures of comet Wild 2 before returning to orbit Earth.

On January 15, 2006, *Stardust*'s collection capsule—which had collected samples from the comet—separated from the main spacecraft and returned to Earth with the help of several parachutes. The main spacecraft was sent into a new orbit around the Sun. *Stardust* flew by Earth on January 14, 2009, and has been picked for an extended mission to the comet Tempel 1 in 2011. Scientists are still busily studying the particles that were returned.

A scientist holds a sample of dust from the Wild 2 comet.

Deep Impact

NASA's *Deep Impact* mission involved sending part of a spacecraft crashing into a comet. Scientists hoped to get a deeper understanding of some of the basic facts about comets. This included finding what makes up the comet's nucleus, measuring the depth of the impact crater, and where the comet was originally formed.

Deep Impact was launched on January 12, 2005, and aimed at the comet Tempel 1. The plan was to have a probe separate from the main spacecraft and strike part of the comet. On July 4, 2005, that probe successfully struck the comet's nucleus, bringing up debris from the inside of the nucleus.

Studies of the material brought to the comet's surface show many different types of elements. Silicates—the family to which sand belongs—that have been heated to crystal and glassy forms were found. Carbon, clay minerals, water (in both ice and gas forms), and sulfides (chemicals containing sulfur) were also found. This combination is similar to the makeup of some other younger comets. Scientists are still analyzing the results of *Deep Impact*'s success.

Deep Impact took this picture as part of the spacecraft crashed into comet Tempel I.

Rosetta

The ESA's *Rosetta* spacecraft, launched in March, 2004, will be the first to undertake a close-up exploration of a comet over a long period of time. *Rosetta* consists of a large orbiter, which is

An illustration shows *Rosetta* deploying the lander that will study Comet 67/P Churyumov–Gerasimenko.

designed to operate for a decade and a small lander. Each of these carries many scientific experiments designed to complete the most detailed study of a comet ever attempted.

It will take ten years for the spacecraft to reach its goal. For much of the long journey, *Rosetta* will remain in hibernation, with its main systems shut down. ESA scientists did "awaken" Rosetta recently, on July 3, 2008, so that it could do a close flyby and observation of the asteroid (2867) Steins on September 5, 2008. After that, the spacecraft went back into hibernation where it will stay until January 2014, when it will finally be in the region of comet 67/P Churyumov-Gerasimenko. At that point, it will attempt a landing and send more data back to Earth.

Future missions, including those that are already in space, will send scientists more information about comets. Scientists hope that learning more about comets will lead to a better understanding of our Solar System, how it was created, and how it is changing.

GLOSSARY

asteroid—A small celestial body that is mostly composed of rock and moves around the Sun, usually between Mars and Jupiter. Asteroids are sometimes called minor planets or planetoids.

celestial object—A natural object in space, such as a planet, moon, star, asteroid, comet, or meteor.

comet—A celestial body made up of a mix of ice, rocks, and dust. A comet has a nucleus and a streaming tail.

Earth-crossing asteroid—An asteroid that comes near Earth, sometimes entering its atmosphere.

flyby—A type of mission that involves having a spacecraft fly close to a celestial object to observe or collect information.

gravity—The force that causes objects to be attracted to each other. Distance and size affect gravitational force.

light-year—A unit of measurement used to measure distances in space. One light-year is equivalent to 5.89 trillion miles (9.46 trillion km).

meteor—Rocky space debris that enters Earth's atmosphere. Meteors can be made up of small asteroids or comet dust. They are often called shooting stars.

meteor shower—A collection of meteors—from comet dust and particles—that streak across the sky. Meteor showers occur when Earth crosses the orbit of a comet.

meteorite—A meteor that has landed on Earth.

meteoroid—Rocky space debris that is smaller than an asteroid and orbits the Sun. Meteoroids become meteors when they enter the Earth's atmosphere.

National Aeronautics and Space Administration (NASA)—The official space agency of the United States.

near-Earth asteroid—An asteroid with an orbit that brings it close to Earth.

orbit—The path taken by a celestial body.

FIND OUT MORE

BOOKS

Barnes-Svarney, Patricia. *A Traveler's Guide to the Solar System*. New York, NY: Sterling Publishing, 2008.

Graham, Ian. *Comets and Asteroids*. North Mankato, MN: Smart Apple Media, 2007.

Way, Jennifer. *Exploring Comets*. New York: PowerKids Press, 2007.

WEBSITES

Asteroids
http://nssdc.gsfc.nasa.gov/planetary/planets/asteroidpage.html

ESA Kids—Asteroids and Meteors
http://www.esa.int/esaKIDSen/SEMCM9WJD1E_OurUniverse_0.html

Halley's Comet
http://www.windows.ucar.edu/tour/link=/comets/Halleys_comet.html

HubbleSite
http://hubblesite.org

NASA Kids' Club
http://www.nasa.gov/audience/forkids/kidsclub/flash/index.html

NASA Solar System Exploration for Kids
http://solarsystem.nasa.gov/kids/index.cfm

NASA—Stardust
http://www.nasa.gov/mission_pages/stardust/main

The Space Place—Catch a Comet!
http://spaceplace.nasa.gov/en/kids/stardust/index.shtml

BIBLIOGRAPHY

The author found these resources especially helpful while researching this book.

Bevan, Alex and John De Laeter. *Meteorites: A Journey Through Space and Time.* Sydney, Australia: The University of New South Wales Press, 2002.

Corfield, Richard. *Lives of the Planets: A Natural History of the Solar System.* New York: Basic Books, 2007.

Lancaster-Brown, Peter. *Halley & His Comet.* Poole, England: Blandford Press, 1985.

Loveday, Veronica. "NASA's NEAR Shoemaker Space Probe Lands on the Asteroid Eros," *Encyclopedia of Science in the Twentieth Century*, 2006 Astronomy, Vol. 2.

Miller, Ron and William K. Hartmann. *The Grand Tour: A Traveler's Guide to the Solar System.* New York: Workman Publishing, 2005.

NASA. "A Virtual Eros." http://www.gsfc.nasa.gov/gsfc/spacesci/near/eros.htm

NASA-NSSDC. "Suisei." http://nssdc.gsfc.nasa.gov/nmc/masterCatalog.do?sc =1985-073A

National Geographic. "Asteroid Belt Discovered Around Our Sun's Twin." http://news.nationalgeographic.com/news/2005/04/0421_050421_spitzer.html

Peebles, Curtis. *Asteroids: A History.* Washington, D.C.: The Smithsonian Institution Press, 2000.

Reynolds, Mike D. *Falling Stars: A Guide to Meteors and Meteorites.* Mechanicsburg, PA: Stackpole Books, 2001.

Yeomans, Donald K. *Comets: A Chronological History of Observation, Science, Myth, and Folklore.* New York: John Wiley and Sons, 1991.

INDEX

ABOUT THE AUTHOR

Josepha Sherman has written everything from fantasy novels to science books to short articles about quantum mechanics for elementary school students.